The
journey
of
prayer

Volumes in the Pathway to the Heart of God Series

PATHWAY TO THE HEART OF GOD

The
journey
of
prayer

TERRY W. GLASPEY

Cumberland House Publishing
Nashville, Tennessee

Published by Cumberland House Publishing, Inc., 431 Harding
Industrial Drive, Nashville, Tennessee 37211

Unless otherwise indicated, verses are taken from the Holy Bible,
New International Version ®, Copyright © 1973, 1978, 1984 by the
International Bible Society. Used by permission of Zondervan
Publishing House. The "NIV" and "New International Version"
trademarks are registered in the United States Patent and
Trademark Office by the International Bible Society.

Cover design by Karen Phillips
Text design by Julia M. Pitkin

Library of Congress Cataloging-in-Publication Data

Glaspey, Terry W.
    The journey of prayer / Terry W. Glaspey
        p. cm. -- (Pathway to the heart of God series)
    ISBN 1-58182-132-8 (hardcover : alk paper)
        1. Prayer--Christianity. 2. Prayer--Christianity--Quotations,
maxims, etc. I. Title

    BV210.2 .G59 2000b
    248.3'2--dc21   00-058989

Printed in the United States of America
1 2 3 4 5 6 7 8 — 05 04 03 02 01 00

contents

introduction

Praying can prove difficult. If this were not the case, we probably wouldn't find prayer to be as hard as we sometimes do. Distractions, confusion about what we should pray for, questions about how our actions should relate to our prayers: These are some of the hurdles we must overcome on the path to a more satisfying life of prayer.

In order to pray faithfully and honestly, it is necessary that we deepen our understanding of prayer and answer for ourselves some of the difficult questions that arise when we think seriously about the act of communicating with God. In this book we will look at the struggle and comfort of prayer, as well as such issues as what it means to "pray without ceasing" and how our prayers relate to the will of God. As we answer some of these questions for ourselves, it will surely draw us closer to the One who is Himself the greatest answer to our prayers.

The book you hold in your hand is the third of four little books about prayer. This particular volume will wrestle with some of the tough questions about prayer, questions that must be answered if our prayer lives are to be what they can be. The other books in the series focus on looking at what prayer really is and how God uses it so powerfully in our lives (*A Time for Prayer*), examining the different elements of a balanced prayer life (*The Joy of Prayer*), and providing practical steps for beginning to make prayer a more integral part of our lives (*The Experience of Prayer*). Each of the four books is a part of the whole. Taken together, their goal is not only to help us understand prayer a little better, but also to inspire us to begin to pray.

Prayer is a topic that continues to be much discussed these days, especially by those who are concerned with making sense of their spiritual lives. There are lots of books around that attempt to explain the ins and outs of what prayer is and how it affects one's life. Some of them claim to have all the answers, to have unlocked some secret key or system for making prayer effective for the reader.

I make no such claim. Like you, I am a learner in the school of prayer. But one of the important

things I have learned is that I am not on my own
when it comes to making sense of this crucial ele-
ment of my spiritual life. Many great thinkers,
writers, theologians, mystics, and activists have
ruminated deeply on this important topic. In this
book, I hope to share a little of what I've learned
from them, mostly in their own words. If, like me,
you realize you have a lot to learn and you truly
desire to make your prayer life more meaningful,
then I invite you to join me in meditating on some
of the most profound and life-changing words ever
written about prayer.

Each year brings a multitude of new books on
prayer. One of the lessons I have learned about
such books is that the most recent ones are not
necessarily the best ones. It seems that a lot of
books published these days are tainted with our
modern materialistic values or our current obses-
sion with the therapeutic sphere. Such books tend
to be more concerned with using prayer as a way
to get what we want or as a method for obtaining
inner peace and tranquility than with learning how
to make communication with God a part of our
honest everyday existence and with growing into
a more intimate relationship with Him.

I invite you, then, to join me on a journey that will sample the thoughts of some of the most insightful believers who ever lived (along with a handful of nonbelievers who thought deeply about the subject). These nuggets of wisdom are best absorbed thoughtfully and slowly, a few at a time. If we are to enter the school of prayer, we must not rush to consider ourselves graduates. Savor these thoughts. Meditate on them. Argue with them. Make them your own.

The writers quoted in this book come from a variety of time periods, religious traditions, cultures, and life experiences. Be forewarned: They do not always agree with each other. Most of the time I have simply allowed their disagreements to stand, expecting the reader to ponder their thoughts with discernment and draw his or her own conclusions. At other times, I have tried to synthesize the various insights together, still endeavoring to avoid the temptation of superficially explaining away the mysteries that will always surround this topic.

Sprinkled in with the text you'll also find some of my favorite prayers from classic writers, many of them composed by the same writers whose thoughts on prayer we will consider. You can use these prayers as models to fashion your own, as inspiration to prepare your heart to pray, or as a way to give voice to concerns and feelings you cannot articulate as well as these saints. You and I can make these prayers our own, for often they can help us express what we would struggle to put into words for ourselves. When prayed with focus and concentration, they can give our hearts wings to fly upward to God.

Finally, I have concluded each section of this book with a prayer I have written. These little prayers are attempts to put the truths of the chapter into practice, for it does us little good to think about prayer or read about praying if we don't actually pray.

I hope you will find this little book to be a helpful companion as you travel your own spiritual path. Think of it as a map you can use as you begin your personal journey into God's heart.

Terry W. Glaspey

The
journey
of
prayer

THE STRUGGLE
OF PRAYER

If we are honest with ourselves, we will admit that the most common reason for prayerlessness in our lives is that we have found prayer to be difficult. It demands time, it demands concentration, and it can sometimes seem like an exercise in futility.

Of course, if we see prayer only as a quaint devotional exercise or as a few words directed heavenward at the end of the day, then prayer is not going to appear difficult at all. If we approach it thoughtlessly, without preparation or serious intention, prayer will seem easy.

But those who have seriously given themselves to prayer are unanimous in testifying that it is hard work. It should not surprise us that prayer is often very difficult. It is serious and eternal work, one of the main tasks God has given to His children. To pray is to overcome our natural tendency to search for quick and painless solutions, to conquer our spiritual sloth.

If we see prayer as a light undertaking, we have failed to grasp the reality that prayer is often a struggle: a struggle with ourselves and a struggle with God.

*Prayer is a kind of
wrestling and contending with God,
a striving with him.*
—RICHARD SIBBES

*True prayer is a struggle with God,
in which one triumphs through
the triumph of God.*
—SÖREN KIERKEGAARD

*Prayer is indeed a continuous
violent action of the spirit as it is lifted up to God.
This action is comparable to that of a ship
going against the stream.*
—MARTIN LUTHER

To pray aright is right earnest work.
—JACOB BOEHME

For a hundred men who are not afraid
or the exertion or labor, there are only a few who
take upon themselves the strain of prayer.
—EMIL BRUNNER

Prayer is the easiest and the hardest
of all things; the simplest and the sublimest;
the weakest and the most powerful; its results lie
outside the range of human possibilities—they are
limited only by the omnipotence of God. Few
Christians have anything but a vague idea
of the power of prayer; fewer still have
any experience of that power.
—E. M. BOUNDS

But this struggle should not be seen as daunting or discouraging. The struggle we experience in prayer is a good thing, for God meets with us in the struggle of prayer.

During that long period,
the king of Egypt died. The Israelites
groaned in their slavery and cried out,
and their cry for help because of their slavery
went up to God. God heard their groaning
and he remembered his covenant with
Abraham, Isaac, and with Jacob.
—EXODUS 2:23

To feed the soul we must toil at prayer.... It is
the assimilation of a holy God's moral strength.
—P. T. FORSYTH

I am worn out from groaning:
all night long I flood my bed with weeping
and drench my couch with tears. My eyes grow
weak with sorrow; they fail because of all my foes.
Away from me, all you who do evil, for the LORD
has heard my weeping. The LORD has heard my
cry for mercy, the LORD accepts my prayer.
—PSALM 6:6-9

Painful and difficult prayer is
more pleasing to God than one which is
easy and tranquil. The grief and pain of one
who tries to pray in vain, lamenting his inability
to do so, makes him a victor in God's sight
and obtains for him abundant graces.
—HENRY SUSO

*Nor is prayer ever heard more abundantly than in
such agony and groanings of a struggling faith.*
—MARTIN LUTHER

In true prayer we pour out the pain and agony
that are resident within our souls. We do not
come to God to impress Him with our holiness,
our theological understanding, or the beauty of
our verbal expression. Rather, we empty ourselves
before God, letting Him know our needs and
desires and allowing our emotional responses be
part of our cry to Him. Tears, cries, groanings, and
other expressions of emotional turmoil are a natural part of the grammar of prayer.

*Trust in him at all times,
0 people; pour out your hearts to him,
for God is our refuge.*
—PSALM 62:8

Arise, cry out in the night,
as the watches of the night begin;
pour out your heart like water in
the presence of the LORD.
—LAMENTATIONS 2:19

During the days of Jesus' life on earth,
he offered up prayers and petitions with
loud cries and tears to the one who could
save him from death, and he was heard
because of his reverent submission.
—HEBREWS 5:7

Usually prayer is a question of groaning
rather than speaking, tears rather than words.
For He sets our tears in His sight, and our groaning
is not hidden from Him who made all things by
His word and does not ask for words of man.
—AUGUSTINE

*Silent prayers are often true prayers,
but there are times, in extremity of suffering,
it is very helpful to give expression to the soul's
agony. I know some friends who can never pray
to their own comfort except they can hear their
own voices; and I believe that it is a good thing for
the most of us to retire to some private place where
we cannot be heard by men, and where we can
therefore freely use our voices in prayer. Very often,
the use of the voice helps to keep the thoughts from
wandering, and also gives intensity to the desires.
You notice that David particularly mentions here
that he cried unto the Lord with his voice. No doubt
many of his prayers ascended to God from his heart
without the medium of his voice; but here, the cry
with voice went with the desires of his heart.*
—CHARLES SPURGEON

*Our prayers must mean something to us
if they are to mean anything to God.*
—MALTBIE D. BABCOCK

*Beloved, what a different view
of prayer God has from that which men
think to be the correct one.... To Him fine
language is as sounding brass or a tinkling
cymbal, but a groan has music in it.*
—CHARLES SPURGEON

The best prayers have often more groans than words.
—JOHN BUNYAN

A groan cometh not from the lips,
but from the heart. A groan then is a
part of prayer which we owe to the Holy
Ghost, and the same is true of all the prayer
which wells up from the deep fountains of our
inner life. The prophet cried, "I am pained at my
very heart: my heart maketh a noise in me." This
deep groundswell of desire, this tidal motion of
the life-floods is caused by the Holy Spirit.
His work is never superficial, but
always deep and inward.
—CHARLES SPURGEON

The dimensions of prayer in solitude
are those of man's ordinary anguish, his
self-searching, his moments of nausea at his
own vanity, falsity and capacity for betrayal.
Far from establishing one in unassailable narcissistic
security, the way of prayer brings us face to face with
the sham and indignity of the false self that seeks
to live for itself and to enjoy the "consolations of
prayer" for its own sake. This self is pure
illusion and ultimately must end either
in disgust or madness.
—THOMAS MERTON

Loving father,
sometimes life can seem so overwhelming.
The pain is so deep,
The confusion so dense,
The struggle so disheartening.
But you, o god, know the full
measure of my anguish.
My feelings are as transparent
to you as my actions.
You have invited me to "be
myself" in prayer,
And so I am free to express the full
intensity of my emotions,
knowing that my honesty opens
the door to healing.
In the name of Him who prayed
for me with all the passion in His soul,
Your son, jesus.
Amen.

PRAYING IN FAITH
AND THE WILL OF GOD

Faith is an essential ingredient in the life of prayer. Without faith, prayer is meaningless. If we do not believe that God will meet us in prayer, then our prayer is no more than an internal dialogue we hold with ourselves.

It is not always easy to believe. There are many forces within us and in the culture around us that would discourage us from believing. It is also hard to believe when we cannot see immediate and verifiable results. But that is what faith is: the unwillingness to be limited to what we can see, and the willingness to believe that there is a reality deeper than the seen world we participate in every day. Faith causes us to look for answers deeper than those available in the earthly realm. It is the trust that God will act on our behalf, whether it be for the salvation of our souls or the meeting of our practical needs.

We must believe in our hearts that God not only cares about us, but that He is capable of reaching out to answer our prayers. It is this confidence that we should have when we come before Him. Such confidence and trust is pleasing to God.

*Without faith it is impossible to please God,
because anyone who comes to him must believe
that he exists and that he rewards those
who earnestly seek him.*
—HEBREWS 11:6

*When he asks, he must believe and not doubt,
because he who doubts is like a wave of the sea,
blown and tossed by the wind.*
—JAMES 1:6

*Prayer is the key of heaven;
faith is the hand that turns it.*
—THOMAS WATSON

*He who prays without confidence
cannot hope that his prayers will be granted.*
—FRANÇOIS FÉNELON

*The possibilities of prayer are the
possibilities of faith. Prayer and faith are
Siamese twins. One heart animates them both.
Faith is always praying. Prayer is always believing.*
—E. M. BOUNDS

*The principal exercise which the
children of God have is to pray; for in this
way they give a true proof of their faith. And
prayer is the inevitable outcome of the presence
of faith in the human heart, for wherever faith
exists, prayer cannot be sluggish.*
—JOHN CALVIN

In the Gospels, we have a record of God's mar-
velous promise that when we pray in faith, He will
answer our prayers.

*If you believe, you will receive
whatever you ask for in prayer.*
—MATTHEW 21:22

*Ask and it will be given to you;
seek and you will find, knock and the door
will be opened to you. For everyone who asks
receives; he who seeks finds, and to him
who knocks, the door will be opened.*
—MATTHEW 7:7

*I tell you the truth, if anyone says to
this mountain, "Go, throw yourself into the sea,"
and does not doubt in his heart but believes that
what he says will happen, it will be done for
him. Therefore I tell you, whatever you ask
for in prayer, believe that you have
received it, and it will be yours.*
—MARK 11:23,24

These verses might seem to promise that we can have whatever we want, that all we have to do is believe with enough vigor. Some people indeed do teach this. They misguidedly claim a promise that, in the words of one contemporary "faith teacher," we can "write our own ticket with God." But, when we balance this with other Scriptures we get a somewhat different picture. Our prayers are answered only so long as they are in agreement with God's will. A heart that hears God seems to be the requirement for receiving whatever we ask for.

*This is the confidence we have
in approaching God: that if we ask anything
according to his will, he hears us.*
—I JOHN 5:14

*If you remain in me
and my words remain in you,
ask whatever you wish,
and it will be given you.*
—JOHN 15:7

So, the mature believer does not treat God as a mail order catalog or as an easy route to success and possessions. Nor does he envision prayer as something akin to the all-request radio station. Instead, he earnestly seeks God's will and prays in accordance with that.

The whole aim of any person who is beginning prayer—and don't forget this, because it's very important—should be that he work and prepare himself with determination and every possible effort to bring his will into conformity with God's will.... It is the person who lives in more perfect conformity who will receive more from the Lord and be more advanced on this road.

—TERESA OF AVILA

Spread out your petition before God, and then say, "Thy will, not mine, be done." The sweetest lesson I have learned in God's school is to let the Lord choose for me.

—DWIGHT L. MOODY

If, seeing we live not by our own will,
we live by another will, then is there reason,
and then only can there be reason in prayer.
—GEORGE MACDONALD

For most of us the prayer
in Gethsemane is the only model.
Removing mountains can wait.
—C. S. LEWIS

Sometimes the most powerful prayer we can pray, then, is the prayer that submits our will to God's.

Is prayer your steering wheel or your spare tire?
—CORRIE TEN BOOM

The most effective kind of prayer
is that in which we place ourselves, in our
hearts, before God, relinquishing all resistance,
letting go of all secret irritation, opening ourselves
to the truth, to God's holy mystery, saying over and
over again, "I desire truth, I am ready to receive it,
even this truth which causes me such concern, if it
be the truth. Give me the light to know it—
and to see how it bears on me."
—ROMANO GUARDINI

The true relation in prayer is not
when God hears what is prayed for, but
when the person praying continues to pray
until he is the one who hears, who
hears what God wills.
—SÖREN KIERKEGAARD

O god,
I have so many desires and dreams,
so many hopes and passions.
But what I desire above all else
is that I might learn to desire only
Your will for my life.
I surrender to Your wisdom.
In Jesus name,
amen.

-3-
THE COMFORT
OF PRAYER

Countless times in my own life I have felt the burdens of my life crowding around me like dark and smothering shadows. Sometimes I have wondered if I could continue to bear up underneath it all. It is in these times of pain that prayer has proven to be the one thing that could keep me going, that could steady my vision, that could bring peace to my heart even while the storms of life swirled about me.

Truly, one of the great things about prayer is the comfort it can bring. It reminds us that God is with us in the midst of all the pains and trials. Just knowing that we can go to Him when no one else can help us or truly understand our pain gives us strength in our time of need. Countless believers can testify to having the experience of feeling that all was lost and dark, only to find hope and strength when they reached out to God in prayer.

I meet with difficulties, disappointments,
humiliations, troubles and temptations of every
kind; if I pray to God to come to my help and give
me strength to bear them, I am asking as I
ought and am therefore entitled to hope
that he will grant my prayer.
—JEAN NICHOLAS GROU

Be not afraid to pray—to pray is right.
Pray, if thou canst, with hope, but ever pray,
Though hope be weak, or sick with long delay;
Pray in the darkness, if there be no light.
—HARTLEY COLERIDGE

Prayer is a remedy against grief and depression.
—NILUS

*Trouble and perplexity drive me to prayer, and
prayer drives away perplexity and trouble.*
—PHILIP MELANCHTHON

*To flee unto God is the only stay
which can support us in our afflictions, the only
armor which renders us invincible.*
—JOHN CALVIN

We can go to friends with our troubles, but so often there is little they can do other than lend a sympathetic ear. It is good that we not suffer alone, but sometimes there is a limit as to what others can do to help us. Even our closest friends oftentimes cannot understand the depths of our difficulties, or the crushing sense of being overwhelmed that overtakes us.

But God is with us in our pain. He knows it deeply and is there to hold us up in the midst of it. The comfort He offers is quiet yet real, calm yet uplifting.

Cast all your cares on God; that anchor holds.
—ALFRED LORD TENNYSON

I waited patiently for the LORD;
he turned to me and heard my cry.
He lifted me out of the slimy pit, out of
the mud and mire; he set my feet on a rock
and gave me a firm place to stand.
He put a new song in my mouth,
a hymn of praise to our God.
—PSALM 40:1-3

In my anguish I cried to the LORD, and he
answered by setting me free.
—PSALM 118:5

Cast all your anxiety upon him
because he cares for you.
—I PETER 5:7

*Let us then approach the throne of grace
with confidence, so that we may receive mercy
and find grace to help us in our time of need.*
—HEBREWS 4:16

Blessed savior,
where would I be without you?
You are my rock in times of trouble,
An eternal spring or refreshment
in a dry and weary land,
The one who will hold me up
when I am near collapse.
You draw near to me in my darkest hours
And set me free from the traps I have
constructed for myself.
Just knowing that you are with me.
Brings light and hope and peace,
Even in times of darkness, despair, and turmoil.
Because of your care for me I rest secure.
Amen.

-4-
PRAYER AND
SPIRITUAL WARFARE

Life is not only a struggle; it is also a war. Throughout Scripture, images of the battlefield are used to describe the sense of conflict that fills our life. When we look around, we see the terrible results of the power of evil. It destroys families, puts individuals and nations at enmity with one another, grapples with us at the point of our greatest weakness, all in an effort to cause us to lose hope.

The Bible clearly teaches us that we have a powerful adversary. Though we are not given a great deal of information about the one who would like to defeat us, we are given a clear picture of his goal: to do whatever is necessary to discourage us in our attempt to live for God. The most important truth about our adversary—the devil, Satan, Beelzebub, he goes by many names—is that he is the enemy of our soul.

The great dragon was hurled down—
that ancient serpent called the devil, or Satan,
who leads the whole world astray.
*—*REVELATION 12:9

We wanted to come to you—
certainly I, Paul, did, again and again—
but Satan stopped us.
*—*1 THESSALONIANS 2:18

Be self-controlled and alert.
Your enemy, the devil prowls around like a
roaring lion looking for someone to devour.
*—*1 PETER 5:8

Simon, Simon, Satan has asked
to sift you as wheat.
—LUKE 22:31

When we begin to pray seriously, we will at times encounter resistance from this enemy. Though some of this resistance can be explained by our own laziness, our sinful nature, our theological confusions, or our inherent selfishness, there are times when we will sense a powerful spiritual force that dissuades us from praying.

We would be foolish to try to fight against such supernatural power in our own strength. The reason Satan does not want us to pray is that prayer is our strongest weapon against him; it is the tool that God has given us to resist his temptations and his incursions into our life.

For this we must know,
that all our shelter and protection rest
in prayer alone. For we are far too feeble
to cope with the devil and all his power and
adherents that set themselves against us, and they
might easily crush us under their feet. Therefore we
must consider and take up those weapons with which
Christians must be armed in order to stand against
the devil. For what do you think has hitherto accom-
plished such great things, has checked or quelled
the counsels, purposes, murder, and riot of our
enemies, whereby the devil thought to crush us,
together with the Gospel, except that the
prayer of a few godly men intervened
like a wall of iron on our side?
　　—MARTIN LUTHER

Prayer is a shield to the soul,
a sacrifice to God and a scourge to Satan.
—JOHN BUNYAN

To clasp the hands in prayer
is the beginning of an uprising
against the disorder of the world.
— KARL BARTH

The old serpent will tempt you
and entice you, but he will be sent packing
by prayer, and if you do some useful work in the
meantime, you will block his chief approach.
—THOMAS À KEMPIS

*The secret prayer chamber is a
bloody battleground. Here violent and
decisive battles are fought out. Here the fate
of souls for time and eternity is determined,
in quietude and solitude.*
—O. HALLESBY

*However great may be the temptation, if
we know how to use the weapon of prayer
well we shall come off conquerors at last, for
prayer is more powerful than all the devils. He
who is attacked by the spirits of darkness needs
only to apply himself vigorously to prayer, and
he will beat them back with great success.*
—BERNARD OF CLAIRVAUX

He who prays must wage a mighty warfare
against the doubt and murmuring excited by
the faintheartedness and unworthiness
we feel within us.
—MARTIN LUTHER

The brethren also asked him,
"Amongst all good works, which is
the virtue which requires the greatest effort?"
He answered, "Forgive me, but I think there is
no labor greater than that of prayer to God. For
every time a man wants to pray, his enemies, the
demons, want to prevent him, for they know that
it is only by turning him from prayer that they
can hinder his journey. Whatever good work
a man undertakes, if he perseveres in it,
he will attain rest. But prayer is
warfare to the last breath."
—AGATHON

To pray is to expose oneself to
the promptings of God; and, by the
same token, to become less suggestible
to the low persuasions of the world.
—GEORGE BUTTRICK

The one concern of the devil
is to keep the saints from praying.
He fears nothing from prayerless studies,
prayerless work, prayerless religion. He
laughs at our toil, he mocks at our wisdom,
but he trembles when we pray.
—SAMUEL CHADWICK

Prayer is that mightiest of all weapons
that created natures can wield.
—MARTIN LUTHER

We must wrestle earnestly in prayer,
like men contending with a deadly
enemy for life.
—J. C. RYLE

Prayer is the great engine to overthrow
and rout my spiritual enemies, the great
means to procure the graces of which
I stand in hourly need.
—JOHN NEWTON

When you pray,
there is a clash of arms in
the heavenly sphere.
—UNKNOWN

Restraining prayer we cease to fight;
Prayer makes the Christian's armour bright;
And Satan trembles when he sees
The weakest saint upon his knees.
—WILLIAM COWPER

Submit yourselves, then,
to God. Resist the devil and
he will flee from you.
—JAMES 4:7

Mighty god,
I feel so helpless in the face of life's battles.
My resistance is so weak,
My resources are so limited.
At times I feel the breath of the evil one
stalking me with the intention of defeating me.
were I left to my own power
I would surely be lost.
But it is not in my own power that I trust
Not in my own ability that I depend.
But it is in the strength that arises
when I invoke the mighty name of Jesus.
Through Him all the darkness
will be put to flight.
Amen.

-5-

PRAYER AND THE SCRIPTURES

Through the ages, believers have found the Scriptures to be indispensable in the walk of faith. The power of the Scriptures to inform, enlighten, and transform has confirmed to many the reality of their claim to be more than just a set of human documents about religion. The Bible claims to be inspired, and the word it uses to speak of that inspiration literally means "God-breathed." Those who have taken the Scriptures seriously can testify to the fact that their narratives and directives are life-changing.

The Bible is a guide for living our lives. We can go to it for understanding, inspiration, and instruction. It testifies to how God related to believers in the past, it helps us understand the great truths that lie behind human existence, and it provides us with practical admonition on how to live out the implications of the good news we have embraced.

One of the great benefits of the Scriptures is that they can strengthen and give structure to our prayer life. Of course the Bible teaches us many truths about prayer, but it is also a tool we can use in our praying. Through thoughtful attention to the many prayers of the Bible, we can learn how better to communicate with God. We can learn to make the words of Scripture a part of our own heartfelt cry. Many of the great Christian writers found the Bible to be a sourcebook of powerful prayers that reflected the deepest feelings of their soul.

*We ought to speak to God
and he wants to hear us, not in the
false and confused speech of our heart, but
in the clear and pure speech which God has
spoken to us in Jesus Christ. God's speech in
Jesus Christ meets us in the Holy Scriptures. If
we wish to pray with confidence and gladness,
then the words of Holy Scripture will have to
be the solid basis of our prayer. For here we
know that Jesus Christ, the Word of God,
teaches us to pray. The words which come
from God become, then, the steps on
which we find our way to God.*
—DIETRICH BONHOEFFER

Turn to the Scripture:
choose some passage that is
simple and fairly practical. Next, come
to the Lord. Come quietly and humbly. There,
before Him, read a small portion of the passage
of Scripture you have opened to.... But in coming
to the Lord by means of "praying the Scripture"
you do not read quickly; you read very slowly.
You do not move from one passage to another,
not until you have sensed the very heart of what
you have read.... If you read quickly, it will you
benefit you little. You will be like a bee that merely
skims the surface of flower. Instead, in this new
way of reading with prayer, you must become
as the bee who penetrates into the depths of
the flower. You plunge deeply within
to remove its deepest nectar.
—MADAME GUYON

[George Mueller describing his devotional hour:] The first thing I did, after having asked in a few words the Lord's blessing upon His precious Word, was to begin to meditate on the Word of God, searching as it were into every verse to get a blessing out of it, not for the sake of the public ministry of the Word, nor for the sake of preaching on what I meditated upon, but for the sake of obtaining food for my own soul. The result I have found to be almost invariably this, that after a very few minutes my soul has been led to confession, or to thanksgiving, or to intercession, or to supplication; so that, though I did not, as it were, give myself to prayer, but to meditation, yet it turned almost immediately more or less into prayer.

—GEORGE MUELLER

Turn the Bible into prayer.
—ROBERT MURRAY MCCHEYNE

The book of Psalms, more than any other book of Scripture, has been the source of many powerful prayers because the Psalms are, in essence, prayers and songs to God. In the Psalms, many Christians have found model prayers that they can pray as their own. Because the Psalms include prayers that reflect seemingly every possible emotional state, we will always find them a fertile source for words that express how we feel in the depths of our hearts. Consider these powerful words of John Calvin about the Psalms:

*There is no emotion anyone will experience
whose image is not reflected in this mirror....
All pains, sorrows, fears, doubts, hopes, cares,
anxieties—in short all the turbulent emotions with
which men's minds are commonly stirred....Thus
is left hidden not one of the very many infirmities
to which we are subject, not one of the very many
vices with which we are stuffed. True prayer is
born first from our own sense of need, then from
faith in God's promises. Here will the readers
be best awakened to sense their ills, and, as well,
to seek remedies for them. Whatever can
stimulate us when we are about to pray
to God, this book teaches.*

—JOHN CALVIN

We cannot bypass the Psalms.
They are God's gift to train us in prayer
that is comprehensive—not patched together
from emotional fragments scattered around
that we chance upon and honest—not a
series of more or less sincere verbal poses
that we think might please our Lord.
—EUGENE PETERSON

Of course, the most famous of all prayers is the prayer that Jesus gave to His disciples as a model for praying, the prayer we usually refer to as "The Lord's Prayer." It is a model prayer because it ties together in one prayer the vital elements of our prayer life. It offers praise, it asks for forgiveness, it makes petition, it addresses our warfare with evil, and it surrenders ultimately to the will of God. It is a prayer that believers of all levels of maturity have found effective for making their prayers whole and complete and for helping them move beyond self-absorption.

This, then, is how you should pray:
"Our Father in heaven,
hallowed be your name,
your kingdom come,
your will be done
on earth as it is heaven.
Give us today our daily bread.
Forgive us our debts,
as we also have forgiven our debtors.
And lead us not into temptation,
but deliver us from the evil one."
—MATTHEW 6:9-13

There is no nobler prayer to be found
upon earth than the Lord's Prayer which
we daily pray because it has this excellent
testimony, that God loves to hear it, which
we ought not to surrender for all the
riches of the world.
—MARTIN LUTHER

*From His goodness in this respect
we derive the great comfort of knowing,
that as we ask almost in His words, we
ask nothing that is absurd, or foreign,
or unreasonable; nothing, in short,
that is not agreeable to Him.*
—JOHN CALVIN

*Cultivate the habit of failing asleep
with the Lord's Prayer on your lips
every evening when you go to bed and
again every morning when you get up.
And if occasion, place, and time permit,
pray before you do anything else.*
—MARTIN LUTHER

*The Lord's Prayer does not
bind us to its form of words
but to its content.*
—JOHN CALVIN

*If you go over all the words of holy prayers,
you will, I believe, find nothing which cannot
be comprised and summed up in the petitions
of the Lord's Prayer. Wherefore, in praying,
we are free to use different words to any
extent, but we must ask the same things.*
—AUGUSTINE

*I am convinced that when
a Christian rightly prays the Lord's Prayer
at any time…his praying is
more than adequate.*
—MARTIN LUTHER

Thank You Father,
That the efficacy of my prayers is not
based upon my own creativity,
my way with words,
or my deep understanding of theology.
"Lord, teach me to pray"
is the cry of my heart.
Thank You that You have
given me models and guides
That I can make my own
And pray back to You the words
You have so graciously provided.
In Jesus,
Amen.

–6–

PRAYING WITHOUT CEASING

Some of the things that Scripture teaches us about prayer are hard to understand. Among the most perplexing of passages is 1 Thessalonians 5:17, which encourages us to "pray without ceasing" (KJV). Most Christians will scratch their head in confusion at such a directive. Pray without ceasing? What exactly does that mean? Are we actually expected to carry out that command? We seem to have a difficult enough time praying regularly and often, without being challenged to pray continually. What, then, are we to make of this scriptural exhortation?

Certainly it does not mean that we are to give up all our responsibilities—our jobs and other activities—to retire into a life of continual prayer. Even monks do not spend all their time on their knees! It also doesn't mean that we can no longer converse with other people because all our time is absorbed in conversing with God. Whatever, then, could Paul have meant when he encouraged believers to "pray without ceasing"? Isn't this an impossibility?

Many of the great writers on prayer would answer, "No." They have suggested that this kind of prayer is achievable if we understand what is meant: that it is not so much a matter of the lips as of the heart. To pray without ceasing, they suggest, is to continually keep our hearts in a state of receptivity to God, with an openness to His love and the aligning of our desires with His will.

It is your heart's desire which is your prayer,
and if your desire continues uninterrupted, so too
does your prayer continue. This is what is meant
by "praying without ceasing": it is the uninterrupted
prayer of the heart. Whatever else you are doing, so
long as your heart desires God, then you never cease
to pray. So if you want to pray without ceasing, you
must always desire God. The continuance of that
desire is the continuance of prayer.
—AUGUSTINE

The principal thing is to stand before God
with the intellect in the heart, and to go on standing
before him unceasingly day and night,
until the end of life.
—THEOPHAN the RECLUSE

When the Spirit has come to reside in
someone, that person cannot stop praying;
for the Spirit prays without ceasing in him. No
matter if he is asleep or awake, prayer is going
on in his heart all the time. He may be eating or
drinking, he may be resting or working—the
incense of prayer will ascend spontaneously
from his heart. The slightest stirring of his
heart is like a voice which sings in silence
and in secret to the Invisible.
—ISAAC THE SYRIAN

Many of the great Christian writers have suggested ways that we can keep ourselves "tuned
into God." It is this mental attunement to God that
they believe Paul had in mind when he spoke of
"praying without ceasing." As we seek to live out
our lives, prayer should stand at the very center of
all our activities.

There is a way of ordering
our mental life on more than one level
at once. On one level we may be thinking,
discussing, seeing, calculating, meeting all the
demands of external affairs. But deep within,
behind the scenes, at a profounder level, we
may also be in prayer and adoration, song
and worship, and a gentle receptiveness
to divine breathings.
—THOMAS KELLY

All our life is like a day of celebration
for us; we are convinced, in fact, that God
is always everywhere. We work while singing,
we sail while reciting hymns, we accomplish
all other occupations of life while praying.
—CLEMENT OF ALEXANDRIA

*There is no Christian who does not
have time to pray without ceasing, But I
mean the spiritual praying, that is: no one
is so heavily burdened with his labor, but that
if he will he can, while working, speak with
God in his heart, lay before Him his need
and that of other men, ask for help, make
petition, and in all this exercise
and strengthen his faith.*
— MARTIN LUTHER

*For perfected souls every place
is to them an oratory, every moment
a time for prayer. Their conversation has
ascended from earth to heaven—that is to
say they have cut themselves off from every
form of earthly affection and sensual
self-love and have risen alone into
the very height of heaven.*
— CATHERINE OF SIENA

Pray frequently and effectually;
I had rather your prayers should
be often than long.
—JEREMY TAYLOR

If anyone should ask me how to carry
out the task of prayer, I would say to him:
Accustom yourself to walk in the presence of
God, keep remembrance of him, and be reverent.
To preserve this remembrance, choose a few short
prayers, or simply take the twenty-four short prayers
of St. John Chrysostom, and repeat them often with
appropriate thoughts and feelings. As you accustom
yourself to this, remembrance of God will bring light
to your mind and warmth to your heart. There is
no way in which you yourself can produce it:
it comes forth direct from God.
—THEOPHAN THE RECLUSE

No one should give the answer
that it is impossible for a man occupied
with worldly cares to pray always. You can
set up an altar to God in your mind by means
of prayer. And so it is fitting to pray at your
trade, on a journey, standing at a counter
or sitting at your handicraft.
—JOHN CHRYSOSTOM

There is no mode of life in the world
more pleasing and more full of delight
than continual conversation with God.
— BROTHER LAWRENCE

Lord,
awaken in us the realization
that we need to call on you continually.
that we need not try to live without your grace.
teach us singleness of purpose.
teach us to have hearts that pray.
teach us to keep ourselves focused on you.
to set up an altar in our hearts,
where our soul might cry out to you continually.
amen.

-7-
TAKING UP THE CHALLENGE

The pages of this book have been filled with insights on prayer, testimonies of its effectiveness, and suggested methods that we might use to improve our prayer lives. Some of these methods and ideas might be new to you, and you may be excited about the prospect of putting them into practice. But if you approach the task with the expectation that the difficulties of prayer will be solved by learning a new technique or gaining a new perception, you will most likely be disappointed. Prayer is hard work. There is no easy shortcut to vibrant prayer.

Disappointment can also arise from thinking that every method will work for every person. But not every insight will be fruitful to every believer. Prayer is individual; as individual as your own personal relationship with God. What was helpful

to one of the great writers of the past may be
ineffective, unworkable, or impractical for you, no
matter how much effort you expend. What is
inspiring and eye-opening to one may be confus-
ing to another. God made each of us unique, and
His ways with us will be as individual as we are.

Find the way of prayer that works best for you.
Often the most natural way of praying will be the
best. For example, my knees tend to wear out
pretty quickly, so I have found that a bracing walk
outdoors creates, for me, a natural environment for
prayer. But just because it is natural or easy doesn't
necessarily mean it is the best path. After all, we
cannot allow ourselves to become lazy when it
comes to spiritual matters. It would be a mistake
to let your prayers be limited by your preferences
or your natural tendencies. It is a good thing to
break out of your accustomed mold. By the same
token, don't always be searching for some new
wrinkle or method. At its heart, prayer is a pretty
simple act. Don't muddy the waters by a search
for the novel or the offbeat.

One of the best ways to improve your prayer
life is by learning more about the focus of your

prayers: God. Read the Scriptures to gain greater understanding of who God is and what He has done for us. Let your thinking about life be shaped by biblical truths, and consequently, your prayers as well. Our prayer lives are often limited or thrown off course by poor theological understanding, but they can be set afire when we gain deeper understanding about God's ways. If we seek God with our minds as well as our hearts, new vistas of understanding will open before us and more focus will be given to our prayers.

As I look back over the pages of this book, I am reminded again of the relevance of the writings of the past for those of us who live in the present. There is much we can learn if we will bend our ears to the insights of the great saints who have preceded us. They challenge us anew not to take lightly the serious task of prayer.

But what should we do with the insights we have gained? If they remain only interesting concepts, if they do not penetrate into our hearts and challenge us, then they have failed to do their work. As Andrew Murray reminds us, prayer is something we learn by doing:

Reading a book about prayer,
listening to lectures, and talking about it
is very good, but it won't teach you to pray.
You get nothing without exercise, without practice.
I might listen for a year to a professor of music
playing the most beautiful music, but that
won't teach me to play an instrument.

Hopefully, the profound thoughts about prayer recorded in this book will help us make the choice to give ourselves to prayer, for prayer begins with a choice: We must choose to involve God in all the various aspects of our life. We won't really begin to make progress in prayer until we decide to take prayer seriously. We may need to do some rearranging of our priorities. Prayer should be one of the major priorities in the life of the believer. Sadly, it often is crowded out by the press of other activities, even our "religious" ones.

When we look into the lives of these great men and women of the past, we see a commitment to prayer. In fact, the strength and unflagging persistence of their prayer lives were such that they sometimes were referred to as the "athletes of prayer" or "prayer warriors." In the same way that an athlete will structure his or her life around the accomplishment of a desired athletic goal—running faster, hitting the ball farther, developing greater endurance, and so on—so did these athletes of prayer make prayer central to their lives. They expended themselves to become better, and more fervent, pra-yers. By doing so, they changed the world.

Are we willing to do the same? Are we willing to restructure our goals, our priorities, and our time around the act of serious prayer? Will we expend the necessary energy to work at becoming more focused in our prayers? Will we make times of prayer a central part of our schedule rather than something we do if we can find the extra time? Are we willing to keep on practicing, to keep on praying, even when it becomes difficult or boring, seems pointless, or seems too emotionally demanding?

All the rich and profound thoughts on prayer, that we have as a legacy from the past, are of no value to us unless they actually cause us to take prayer more seriously.

And we should take prayer seriously.

Any way we look at it, prayer is an awesome privilege. To think that the creator of all things

desires to hear about all our needs and concerns
is a staggering thought. Seen from an eternal per-
spective, the matters that concern us are, for the
most part, rather trivial. Who are we that God
should bother to hear us? And yet, God does not
hold our concerns to be trivial. The wonder of it
all is that God is willing to concern Himself with
what concerns us. That He is willing, and in fact
desirous, to lend an ear to our problems and strug-
gles reveals a great deal about our relationship
with Him and His love for us.

Love is God's motivation for giving us the gift of
prayer. It should also be our prime motivation in
praying. We do not pray primarily to receive whatever it is we think we need, or to fulfill what we
perceive to be our religious duty. We pray because
we love God. We pray because our hearts cry out
from their need to communicate with Him. We
pray because we desire His companionship with
us on the pathway of life.

God is not an impersonal metaphysical force or
an indifferent "supreme being." He has revealed
Himself to be a lover—one who wants to be in
relationship with His creatures. He is the source
of all life and the giver of every good gift, even

those gifts that may not seem good to us at the time we receive them. He is infinite, but He is also personal.

Prayer is the most intimate activity we can share with God. I do not think it is too much of a stretch to suggest that prayer is to our relationship with God what the sexual relationship is to a healthy marriage. It is the utmost in self-revelation, where we bare our hearts before God. In prayer we reveal our true selves and make ourselves vulnerable to God. We spend our passion in pursuing His pleasure. We long for His presence with us and in us.

As we undertake the life of prayer, then, it is important that we keep our eyes on what really matters. We should focus not on the methods of prayer, but on the One to whom we pray. A heart that pants for God as a deer pants for water (Psalm 42:1) is the foundation of true prayer. We pray because we long to be in communication with God. We want to speak, to pour out our hearts, to be heard. The glory of prayer is that we can be, in a sense, face to face with God, even as Adam was in the garden when God walked with him "in the cool of the day." Prayer truly is the pathway to the very heart of God!

-8-

fAMOUS PRAYERS AND
PRAYERS OF THE fAMOUS

Our prayers need not be beautifully articulated or theologically profound to receive an answer from God. He appreciates the honest outpourings of our heart. Our words are precious to Him. But, from those who have expressed themselves well in their praying, perhaps much more clearly than we are capable of ourselves, we can learn the discipline of thinking carefully and praying seriously.

Come near to the holy men and women of the past and you will soon feel the heat of their desire after God. They mourned for Him, they prayed and wrestled and sought for Him day and night, in season and out, and when they had found Him the finding was all the sweeter for the long seeking.
—A. W. TOZER

I have gathered together a collection of some well-known "written" prayers, many composed by the same writers whose thoughts on prayer we have considered.

We can use these prayers as models to fashion our own prayers, inspirations to prepare our hearts to pray, or ways to give voice to concerns and feelings that we cannot articulate. We can make these prayers our own, for sometimes they will help us to express what we struggle to put into words for ourselves. When prayed with focus and concentration they can give our hearts wings to fly upward to God.

Lord, end my winter, and let my spring begin.
I cannot with all my longing raise my soul out
of her death and dullness, but all things are
possible with Thee. I need celestial influences,
the clear shinings of Thy love, the beams of
Thy grace, the light of Thy countenance, these
are the Pleiades to me. I suffer much from sin and
temptation, these are my wintry signs, my terrible
Orion. Lord, work wonders in me, and for me.
—CHARLES SPURGEON

Open wide the window of our spirits,
O Lord, and fill us full of light;
Open wide the door of our hearts, that we may
receive and entertain Thee with all our powers
of adoration and love. Amen.
—CHRISTINA ROSSETTI

God grant us,
the serenity to accept the things we cannot change,
the courage to change the things we can,
and the wisdom to know the difference. Amen.
—REINHOLD NIEBUHR

*My Lord God, I have no idea where
I am going, I do not see the road ahead
of me, I cannot know for certain where it
will end. Nor do I really know myself and
the fact that I think I am following Your will
does not mean that I am actually doing so. But
I believe that the desire to please You does in fact
please You. And I hope that I will never do anything
apart from that desire. And I know that if I do this
You will lead me by the right road, though I may
know nothing about it. Therefore I will trust You
always though I may seem to be lost and in the
shadow of death. I will not fear for You are
ever with me, and You will never leave
me to face my perils alone.*
—THOMAS MERTON

*Lord, I know not what I ought to ask of You.
You only know what I need. You know me
better than I know myself, O Father, give to Your
child what he himself knows not how to ask.
Teach me to pray. Pray Yourself in me.*
—FRANCOIS FÉNELON

O Lord, I have heard a good word
inviting me to look away to Thee and be
satisfied. My heart longs to respond, but sin
has clouded my vision till I see Thee but dimly.
Be pleased to cleanse me in Thine own precious
blood, and make me inwardly pure, so that I may
with unveiled eyes gaze upon Thee all the days of
my earthly pilgrimage. Then shall I be prepared
to behold Thee in full splendor in the day when
Thou shalt appear to be glorified in Thy saints
and admired in all them that believe. Amen.
—A. W. TOZER

Make us worthy, Lord,
to serve others throughout the world
who live and die in poverty and hunger,
Give them, through our hands, this day
their daily bread,
and by our understanding love,
give peace and joy.
—MOTHER TERESA

Lord, make me an instrument of Your peace
where there is hatred, let me sow love;
where there is injury, pardon;
where there is doubt, faith;
where there is despair, hope;
where there is darkness, light,
and where there is sadness, joy.
0 Divine Master,
grant that I may not so much seek
to be consoled as to console,
to be understood, as to understand,
to be loved, as to love.
For it is in giving that we receive,
it is in pardoning that we are pardoned,
and it is in dying that we are born to eternal life.
            —FRANCIS OF ASSISI

Teach me, Lord, to sing of Your mercies.
Turn my soul into a garden, where the flowers
dance in the gentle breeze, praising You with
their beauty. Let my soul be filled with beautiful
virtues; let me be inspired by Your Holy Spirit;
let me praise You always.
            —TERESA OF AVILA

*The house of my soul is too small for You
to come to it. May it be enlarged by You. It is
in ruins: restore it. In Your eyes it has offensive
features. I admit it, I know it; but who will clean
it up? Or to whom shall I cry other than You?
"Cleanse me from my secret faults, Lord, and
spare Your servant from sins to which I
am tempted by others"—Psalm 31.5.*

—AUGUSTINE

*Blessed are your saints, O Lord,
who have traveled over the rough sea
of this life, and have reached the harbor
of eternal peace and joy. Watch over us
who are still on the dangerous voyage. Our
ship is frail, and the ocean is wide. But in
Your mercy You have set us on our course
with Your Son as our pilot, guiding us
towards the everlasting shore of peace,
the quiet haven of our hectic desire.*

—AUGUSTINE

Lord, look at my soul's wounds.
Your living and effective eye sees everything.
It pierces like a sword,
even to part asunder soul and spirit.
Assuredly, my Lord,
You see in my soul the traces of my former sin;
my present perils, and also motives
and occasions for others to see also.
You see these things, Lord,
and I would have You see them.
You know well, O searcher of my heart,
that there is nothing in my soul that
I would hide from You,
even had I the power to escape Your eyes....
Lord, may Your good, sweet Spirit
descend into my heart,
and fashion there a dwelling for Himself
cleansing it from all defilement
both of flesh and spirit,
pouring into it the increment
of faith, hope and love,
disposing it to penitence and love and gentleness.
—AELRED OF RIEVAULX

I do need Thee, Lord. I need Thee now.
I know that I can do without many things that
once I thought were necessities, but without Thee I
cannot live, and I dare not die. I needed Thee when
sorrow came, when shadows were thrown across the
threshold of my life, and Thou didst not fail me then.
I needed Thee when sickness laid a clammy hand
upon my family and I cried to Thee, and Thou didst
hear. I needed Thee when perplexity brought me to
a parting of the ways, and I knew not how to turn.
Thou didst not fail me then, but in many ways, big
and little, didst indicate the better way. And though
the sun is shining around me today, I know that I
need Thee even in the sunshine, and shall still need
Thee tomorrow. I give Thee my gratitude for that
constant sense of need that keeps me close to thy
side. Help me to keep my hand in Thine and my
ears open to the wisdom of Thy voice. Speak to me,
that I may hear Thee giving me courage for hard
times and strength for difficult places; giving me
determination for challenging tasks. I ask of Thee
no easy way, but just Thy grace that is sufficient for
every need, so that no matter how hard the way,
how challenging the hour, how dark the sky, I may
be enabled to overcome. In Thy strength, who hast
overcome the world, I make this prayer. Amen.
—PETER MARSHALL

Almighty God,
Father of our Lord Jesus Christ,
Maker of all things, Judge of all men;
We acknowledge and bewail our manifold
sins and wickedness, which we, from time to
time, most grievously have committed, by thought,
word and deed, against Thy Divine Majesty,
provoking most justly Thy wrath and indignation
against us. We do earnestly repent, and are heartily
sorry for these our misdoings. The remembrance of
them is grievous unto us, the burden of them is
intolerable. Have mercy upon us, have mercy upon
us, most merciful Father. For Thy Son our Lord
Jesus Christ's sake, forgive us all that is past, and
grant that we may ever hereafter serve and please
Thee in newness of life. To the honour and glory of
Thy name. Through Jesus Christ our Lord. Amen.
—THE BOOK OF COMMON PRAYER

Come Lord, set us on fire.
Clasp us close to Your bosom.
Seduce us with Your beauty.
Enchant us with Your fragrance.
Let us love You.
-AUGUSTINE

God be in my head, and in my understanding;
God be in my eyes, and in my looking,
God be in my mouth, and in my speaking,
God be in my heart, and in my thinking;
God be at my end, and at my departing.
—TRADITIONAL IRISH PRAYER

The Lord pour out His Spirit upon us
that every chamber of our nature may be
sweetened and perfumed with the indwelling
of God, till our imagination shall only delight
in things chaste and pure, till our memory shall
cast out the vile stuff from the dark chambers;
till we shall expect and long for heavenly things,
and our treasure shall all be in heaven and our
heart be there. Take our highest manhood, Lord,
and saturate it in Thy love, till like Gideon's
fleece it is filled with dew, every lock and
every single fleck of it, not a single
portion of it left unmoistened
by the dew from heaven.
—CHARLES SPURGEON

Open the eyes of our hearts to know Thee,
who alone art Highest, amid the highest, and
ever abidest Holy amidst the holy. Thou dost
bring down the haughtiness of the proud, and
scatterest the devices of the people. Thou settest
up the lowly on high, and the lofty Thou does
cast down. Riches and poverty, death and life,
are in Thine hand; Thou alone art the discerner
of every spirit, and the God of all flesh. Thine eyes
behold the depths and survey the works of man;
Thou art the aid of those in peril, the saviour of them
that despair, the creator and overseer of everything
that hath breath.... Do Thou deliver the afflicted,
pity the lowly, raise the fallen, reveal Thyself to
the needy, heal the sick, and bring home Thy
wandering people. Feed Thou the hungry,
ransom the captive, support the weak, comfort
the faint-hearted. Let all the nations of the
earth know that Thou art God alone,
that Jesus Christ is Thy child, and that
we are Thy people and the sheep
of Thy pasture.
—CLEMENT OF ROME

As my body without my soul is a carcass,
so is my soul without Thy Spirit a Chaos, a
dark, obscure heap of empty faculties; ignorant
of itself, unsensible of Thy goodness, blind to Thy
glory; dead in sins and trespasses. Having eyes I
see not, having ears I hear not, having a heart
I understand not the glory of Thy works and the
glory of Thy Kingdom. O Thou Who art the root
of my being and the Captain of my salvation,
look upon me. Quicken me, O Thou life-giving
and Quickening seed. Visit me with Thy light
and Thy truth; let them lead me to Thy Holy Hill
and make me to see the greatness of Thy love in
all its excellencies, effects, emanations, gifts, and
operations. O my Wisdom! O my Righteousness,
Sanctification, and Redemption! Let Thy wisdom
enlighten me, let Thy knowledge illuminate me,
let Thy blood redeem me, wash me and clean me,
let Thy merits justify me, O Thou Who art equal
unto God, and didst suffer for me. Let Thy
righteousness clothe me. Let Thy will imprint the
form of itself upon mine; and let my will become
conformable to Thine, that Thy will and mine
may be united, and made one forevermore.

—THOMAS TRAHERNE

Now I lay me down to sleep,
I pray Thee, Lord, my soul to keep;
If I should die before I wake,
I pray Thee, Lord, my soul to take.
—NEW ENGLAND PRIMER

The prayers I make will then be sweet indeed,
If Thou the spirit give by which I pray:
My unassisted heart is barren clay,
That of its native self can nothing feed.
Of good and pious works Thou art the seed,
That Quickens only where Thou sayest it may;
Unless Thou show to us Thine own true way,
No man can find it: Father! Thou must lead.
Do Thou, then, breathe those thoughts into my mind
By which such virtue may in me be bred,
That in Thy holy footsteps I may tread;
The fetters of my tongue do Thou unbind,
That I may have the power to sing of Thee
And sound Thy praises everlastingly.
—MICHELANGELO

Brief Biographies of Quoted Writers

AELRED OF RIEVAULX (1109–1167) English church leader.

AGATHON (unknown) Early church monk, desert father.

AUGUSTINE (345–430) Early African bishop and prolific writer.

MALTBIE D. BABCOCK (1858–1901) American pastor and poet.

KARL BARTH (1888–1968) Swiss theologian.

BERNARD OF CLAIRVAUX (1090–1153) Medieval spiritual leader and writer.

JACOB BOEHME (1575–1624) Protestant mystical writer.

E. M. BOUNDS (1835–1913) Popular writer of many books on prayer.

EMIL BRUNNER (1889–1966) Swiss theologian.

JOHN BUNYAN (1628–1688) English writer of *Pilgrim's Progress* and other books.

GEORGE BUTTRICK (1892–1980) Anglo–American pastor and devotional writer.

JOHN CALVIN (1509–1564) French reformer and systematic theologian.

CATHERINE OF SIENNA (1347–1380) Mystic, church leader

SAMUEL CHADWICK (1860–1932) English church leader.

JOHN CHRYSOSTOM (c. 345–407) Greek church father known as "golden mouth" for his oratorical skills.

CLEMENT OF ALEXANDRIA (c. 150–215) Early church writer and philosopher.

CLEMENT OF ROME (died . 101) One of the Apostolic Fathers.

WILLIAM COWPER (1731–1800) English poet.

FRANÇOIS FÉNELON (1651–1715) French mystical writer.

P. T. FORSYTH (1848–1921) Scottish theologian and writer.

FRANCIS OF ASSISI (1182–1226) Beloved saint and reformer. Founder of Franciscan order of monks.

JEAN NICHOLAS GROU (1731–1803) French mystical writer.

MADAME GUYON (1648–1717) French mystic, founder of Quietist movement.

O. HALLESBY (1879–1961) Norwegian theologian.

THOMAS KELLY (1893–1941) American theologian and devotional writer.

THOMAS À KEMPIS (1380–1471) Monastic author of *The Imitation of Christ.*

SÖREN KIERKEGAARD (1853–1855) Danish philosopher and theologian.

BROTHER LAWRENCE (c. 1605–1691) Monk and mystical writer.

C. S. LEWIS (1898–1963) English professor, prolific writer, and Christian apologist.

MARTIN LUTHER (1482–1546) German founder of the Reformation, author of numerous treatises, commentaries, and devotional books.

GEORGE MACDONALD (1824–1904) Scottish minister, novelist, and poet.

ROBERT MURRAY MCCHEYNE (1813–1843) Scottish minister.

PHILIP MELANCHTHON (1497–1560) German scholar and reformer alongside Luther.

THOMAS MERTON (1915–1968) American monk and mystical writer.

MICHELANGELO (1475–1564) Italian painter and sculptor.

DWIGHT L. MOODY (1837–1889) American preacher-evangelist.

MOTHER TERESA (1910-1997) Yugoslavian nun and missionary to India.

GEORGE MUELLER (1805–1898) German philanthropist, founder of numerous orphanages in Britain.

ANDREW MURRAY (1828–1917) South African devotional writer.

REINHOLD NEIBUHR (1893–1971) American theologian and writer.

JOHN NEWTON (1725–1807) English hymn writer.

NILUS (unknown) Early church monk, desert father.

EUGENE PETERSON (1932–   ) American pastor and writer.

CHRISTINA ROSSETTI (1830–1894) English poet.

J. C. RYLE (1816–1900) English bishop and writer.

CHARLES SPURGEON (1834–1892) Gifted English preacher and writer.

HENRY SUSO (c. 1300–1366) German mystical writer.

JEREMY TAYLOR (1613–1667) English bishop and writer.

CORRIE TEN BOOM (1892–1983) Concentration camp survivor and writer.

ALFRED LORD TENNYSON (1809–1892) English poet.

TERESA OF AVILA (1515–1592) Spanish mystic, writer, and church reformer.

THEOPHAN THE RECLUSE (1815–1894) Eastern Orthodox bishop and scholar.

A. W. TOZER (1897–1963) American pastor and devotional writer.

THOMAS TRAHERNE (1637–1674) English poet.

THOMAS WATSON (c. 1686) English theologian and preacher.

Terry Glaspey is an editor and an author of several significant books, including *Your Child's Heart, Not a Tame Lion: The Spiritual Legacy of C. S. Lewis,* and *Great Books of the Christian Tradition*. He lives in Eugene Oregon.

Theophan — 79